Creative Music, Kids, and Christian Education

by Mary Ingram Zentner

Augsburg Fortress

Contents

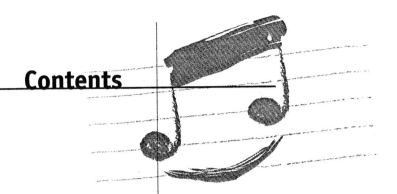

CREATIVE MUSIC, KIDS,
AND CHRISTIAN EDUCATION
by Mary Ingram Zentner

Editors: Susan R. Niemi and
Elizabeth Drotning
Cover: Marti Naughton
Interior design: Mike Mihelich
Illustrator: Brian Jensen
Photos: © 2002 PhotoDisc

ISBN 0-8066-6405-3

Manufactured in the U.S.A.

Introduction

Musical compositions created and performed by learners in your faith community can have a powerful impact on their understanding of God's word. These musical compositions do not need to be limited to traditional instruments and notation. Sounds found around us and within us can be used to explore the timeless stories of God's people.

Creative music uses many of the elements and concepts of traditional music. Concepts such as loud and soft, fast and slow, and long and short are important for learners to consider as they create a composition. By removing the need for exact pitch and rhythm notation, more learners can enter into the process of composing and performing instrumental pieces. The important thing is that they are involved in the creation.

Imagine the grin on Josh's face as the performance of his first musical composition ends. The composition consists of sounds he chose, grouped together, and placed in a particular order to convey what he felt was important from the story of the Israelites crossing the Red Sea. Josh's choice of fast finger tapping and feet stamping makes it easy to imagine the urgency felt by the Israelites as they tried to outrun the Egyptians. The five seconds of silence at the end gives the listener time to exhale from relief for the Israelites. When Josh and his classmates finished performing his composition, all the performers were proud of their accomplishments.

This book looks at what creative music is and how it can be used in Christian education programs that value a variety of ways to allow learners to explore God's word. It encourages the exploration of the many sounds we hear and make in our world. Connections are made between sounds and their use in communicating events and feelings found in Bible stories. The book also guides the leader to facilitate creative music activities with children of all ages.

Open your eyes, your ears, your mind, and your body to the wonders of creative music in God's world. May the sound of God's word never seem the same to you again!

Chapter 1

What Is Creative Music?

Which of the following are examples of creative music?

➤ Carlos stood by the piano in the corner of the church basement. He could hear the thunderstorm outside. After every clap of thunder he rolled his knuckles several times over the lower piano keys, making a loud, rumbling sound. Sometimes he would try to imitate the rain by gently tapping on several piano keys at the higher end of the piano.

➤ Mike and Angie were waiting in the car while their mom filled the gas tank at the gas station. Mike pulled the new bag of candy from the grocery bag and started shaking it. Angie grabbed a pencil and tapped it against the window. They tried various rhythms and answered each other's sounds.

➤ Mr. and Mrs. Grover's third grade Sunday school class enjoys singing "Jesus Loves Me" and making up extra verses.

➤ Kaya was humming as she moved around the yard, flapping her arms. When her arms were high in the air, you could hear her voice go as high as it could go. When her flapping arms came down, her voice went very low.

➤ Mai plays her favorite violin solo as her friend Betsy dances around the room, creating a dance to the music Mai is playing. They decide to do it for their friends Scott, Maria, and Kim. When Mai and Betsy perform, their friends are excited about what they hear and see.

Did you guess that all of the stories were examples of creative music? Did some examples surprise you?

I like to add the word *creative* when I want people to think beyond what many think of as music. Music is an important part of our lives and culture. If you asked a group of people to describe music, they might respond by listing quite a few things. They might describe some of the elements of music such as melody, rhythm, and harmony. They might describe different forms of music such as songs or hymns, orchestral music, band music, symphonies, operas, or choral music. Others might focus on styles of music such as rock, jazz, country, folk, rap, and so on. They might also describe things we do such as singing, playing an instrument, or listening to music.

How many would describe something like what Carlos, Mike, Angie, and Kaya were doing as music? Yet exploring sounds, arranging certain types of sounds in a particular order, and moving our bodies in response to sounds are all part of music.

Putting the word *creative* in front of music helps us go beyond what we typically hear on the radio, television, in church, and on recordings. It also helps to remind us that music is an art form that invites us to be involved. We can be a part of the creative process. It is not something that is just done to us. It is something that happens with us.

CREATIVE MUSIC IN ACTION

Traditionally there are six skills that children are taught when learning music. A balanced program includes all six, allowing children to learn in a variety of ways. These six skills are important to remember as you plan and implement music learning related to Bible stories. They provide a path for children to explore the many facets of a Bible story. Let's look at the six skills in the context of creative music.

➢ *Singing.* Go beyond the singing of melodies and harmonies. Consider the variety of sounds the human voice can make. How do our voices express fear, worry, sadness, joy, excitement, and so forth?

➢ *Playing.* Playing an instrument, including traditional rhythm instruments, can be great fun. Consider other ways to play "traditional instruments" and the many sounds that are available in your home, church, outdoors, and so forth. Remember Mike and Angie!

➢ *Moving.* For some learners, moving their bodies in response to music can be the most satisfying of all music activities. Moving can have value in providing opportunities for personal expression, learning concepts, and understanding characters in stories. Let your learners imagine and explore the many ways their bodies move in response to sound and story.

➢ *Listening.* Because music is made up of sound, listening is very important. We listen to both the sounds we create and the sounds others create. Real listening is a skill that is learned. Help learners listen carefully to the many sounds around them. What do they hear when combine sounds in various ways?

➢ *Creating.* Creating something of your own is perhaps the most personal experience of all. Your "piece" might be very simple, complex, or something in between. It doesn't really matter. What does matter is that you have the opportunity to organize sounds in a way that you want.

➢ *Reading.* Think beyond traditional musical notes and notation. How would Carlos write down what he was doing on the piano during the thunderstorm? How could he communicate it so others could do it, too? How could he notate it so that he could remember what he did and reproduce it at a later time? Squiggles, pictures, and other symbols can help us notate the sounds we choose.

One Christmas a number of my relatives were gathered at my parents' home. A few of us decided to sing Christmas carols. I played the piano while the others gathered around me. One of my cousins and I decided to sing my mom's favorite Christmas hymn. We were the only ones who knew it in the language it was originally written. My cousin apologized before we started singing, saying he wasn't very good at singing. I try very hard to ignore statements like that from people, and so we forged ahead. At the end of the hymn I turned to him and commented that he had a very nice voice. Every note was on pitch. How sad that he had spent approximately 50 years of his life believing a teacher who told him (when he was young) that he couldn't sing.

PERFORMERS AND AUDIENCES: WE'RE IN THIS TOGETHER

The six skills previously listed provide a way for everyone to be active in a variety of musical experiences. But not everyone feels comfortable with the idea of being active when it comes to music. This can be especially true of adults.

We have heard countless talented musicians on recordings, on stage, in movies and television programs. And that's just the professionals! What about the soloist at church, the choir director at school, the local piano teacher, friends, neighbors, and even your Aunt Sally? Perhaps they have spent years practicing singing or playing an instrument. They may even appear comfortable getting up in front of a group of people and performing.

Does all of this talent, skill, and experience make you (or someone you know) nervous? Does it make you feel less talented because you can't do the same things? Or maybe you're one of the unfortunate ones who has had someone tell you to just mouth the words when singing in a group since you couldn't match all of the pitches correctly to the song.

One of my goals in getting people involved in creative music is to break down the idea that there are two classifications of people:

➤ those who have some extraordinary musical talent and have cultivated that talent to become accomplished musicians, and

➤ the rest of us.

These two classifications give way to the few who perform and the majority who are the audience for them. My view is that everyone should have the opportunity to explore music, sounds, and movement. This is especially true for children. In creative music the process is very important. The end results can be important, too. But what is learned in the process is key.

COMBINING ALL KINDS OF MUSIC

Think about the kinds of music you already do with children in your church. Do you have a children's choir? Does someone teach the Sunday school children songs and hymns? These are great. Keep doing them. Check to see how many of the six skills listed above are present in the music activities you already do.

Creative music does not advocate getting rid of traditional music. Instead, it can enrich what is already being done and add elements to learning and expression for children.

Let me give you an example of how you can combine all kinds of music. Take the story of Noah and the flood. It's a very popular story and so there are several songs that already exist. Children could learn such songs as "Rise and Shine," "One More River," and "Who Built the Ark?" These songs have quite a few verses. One option is to write additional verses to the songs. You might also take a popular melody ("Twinkle, Twinkle, Little Star" or "Jesus Loves Me") and write your own words to tell the story. A third option is to explore what it might have sounded like as it began to rain. The rain got heavier and continued for a

long time. Eventually there was so much rain that the ark began to float. Choose "found" sounds (see Chapter 4) and create and perform a "rain composition." Add in movements to the composition.

All three options allow learners to develop several different types of skills and be involved in learning. Some of the activities help tell the story and help learners remember the story. Other activities help them to imagine being there when the story took place. They are in a rainstorm. They might begin to understand how it felt to hear nothing but rain and wind. Above all, have fun discovering something new when you combine different kinds of music and sound.

Creative music can be both fun and a valuable learning experience. It is designed to take away some of the performance anxiety and fear of failure associated with music. A key element is to try something and see how it works. If it doesn't work, then new ideas are tried. It also works well with already existing musical compositions. Give it a try and see what happens!

Creative Music and Christian Education

When's the last time you listened to or sang a song of praise to God? When's the last time you turned to the psalms when you were feeling discouraged? Throughout history, people of faith have used music to express their relationship with God. They used music to praise, lament, thank, encourage, and tell stories.

MUSIC IN BIBLE TIMES

Both secular and sacred music were important in the lives of people of biblical times. If you were to travel back in time, what would you hear and see?

➤ Psalms were sung and prayed in synagogues.

➤ People danced at weddings and other celebrations. (Men and women danced separately.)

➤ Cymbals, both loud cymbals and high-sounding cymbals, were used in worship.

➤ A *kinnor* was the small eight- or ten-stringed lyre used by David. It was played using fingers or a pick.

➤ A small drum called a timbrel was played by women. The timbrel was made from two skins stretched over a wooden hoop.

➤ In the time of Moses, trumpets or horns were played by the priests to signal the people to break camp or come together. They also sounded the trumpets while offering sacrifices to God at special festivals.

➤ The *shofar* or ram's horn is the most frequently mentioned biblical instrument and is still in use today in synagogues. It can only produce two or three notes. The shofar was used for signaling in times of war and in national celebrations.

➤ The *nebel* was a type of harp. It is usually mentioned along with the lyre in the Bible.

➤ A noisemaker had a wooden frame with wires across it. The wires had metal disks on them. When shaken, the disks rattled. These have been translated as "castanets," "rattles," "sistrums," or "clappers."

➤ A *khalil* is a type of flute or pipe. It was generally used on joyful occasions, but was also suitable for mourning.

➤ The people sometimes shouted during worship as a way to praise God.

➤ A choir and an orchestra were present during David's time. The orchestra had horns, trumpets, harps, and cymbals. Both were used in worship.

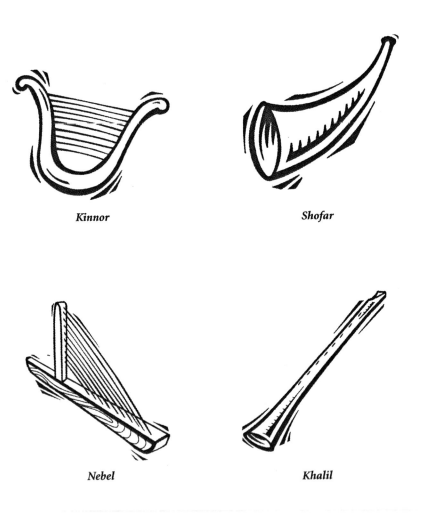

Kinnor

Shofar

Nebel

Khalil

RESPONDING TO LIFE AROUND US

What's been happening in your life lately? Have you or anyone you know written a psalm in response to what's been happening? It could be short or long, written words or with a melody added. You might have tapped out a rhythm on a table to accompany what you created.

One response we are to give is to praise God. The psalms are full of examples of praising God by using music.

Sing joyfully

Sing joyful songs to the LORD!
Praise the mighty rock
where we are safe.

Psalm 95:1

Create something new

Sing a new song to the LORD!
Everyone on this earth,
sing praises to the LORD

Psalm 96:1

Worship God with song

Come to worship him
with thankful hearts
and songs of praise

Psalm 95:1

Use instruments, move to music

Praise God with trumpets
and all kinds of harps.
Praise him with tambourine
and dancing,
with stringed instruments
and woodwinds.
Praise God with cymbals,
with clashing cymbals.

Psalm 150:3-5

God's people through the ages have responded to life around them with music. Miriam created a song of praise, recorded in Exodus 15, extolling the wondrous things God did to save the Israelites as they fled from Egypt. She and the other women took their tambourines out and played and danced, singing praises to God. They must have treasured their tambourines to include them in their belongings as they made their exit. Miriam's song of praise was created on the spot, accompanied by what the women had with them. The people were creative in their response to what had just happened to them.

Music is an important means to express our feelings as we respond to life around us. Psalmists in the past have expressed desire for forgiveness (Psalms 51 and 106), trust when things aren't going well (Psalms 69, 61, 58, 37), and deep despair (Psalms 22, 38, 109). You, too, can create words, sounds, and melodies to express your feelings and share them with God and others.

When in Philippi, Paul and Silas found themselves in jail (Acts 16). First their clothes were torn off; then they were beaten with a whip. They were put deep inside the jail and chained to the stocks. Then what did Paul and Silas do? At midnight they were praying and singing praises to God! Was it a way to get past the pain and focus on the positive, on someone greater than them? Probably. With all that had happened, they needed to encourage one another. Music played a part in it. It's doubtful there were any musical instruments in the jail. So they did what they could with what they had.

RESPONDING TO GOD'S WORD WITH CREATIVE MUSIC

We've looked at the way people of faith used music and found examples of ways to incorporate music as we seek to live as children of God. We have seen how music can be used to offer praise and thanksgiving to God and to tell the story of what God has done.

Creative music also can help us explore the feelings of the characters in Bible stories. How did the Israelites feel when they found manna for the first time? There might have been mixed feelings that require different sounds to help express what was going on. How might we use sound to try to describe Mary and Martha? What different sounds could we use to describe two women who were different in some ways but alike in others? How might the widow have felt as she gave her last penny? Was she joyful, worried, or a little of both?

Creative music can help us express our feelings when we read Bible stories. We can explore feelings that might be similar to or different from the characters in the story. Whatever our response, music is one way to express our experience.

> *Music is an important means to express our feelings as we respond to life around us.*

Sometimes composers write music to convey a story using only sounds and pitches. They attempt to create images and sequences of events without using words or pictures. Creative music can be used by learners of all ages to convey a biblical story. What sound or combination of sounds could be used to depict the robber attack in the good Samaritan story? How might the sounds be different when the good Samaritan came along to help the man? If you put the sounds together in a sequence and you know the story, you can imagine the sequence of events by listening to the sounds.

It's fun to imagine the kinds of sounds that people in Bible stories might have heard when the story took place. Older learners enjoy researching what life was like at the time. By learning what happened at the temple in Jerusalem, learners could list what sounds Jesus and his disciples heard while they were there. By learning who traveled the roads, learners could reproduce the sounds those on the road to Emmaus might have heard in the background.

There are many ways to explore Bible stories with sound, music, and movement. In chapter 3, we'll look more specifically at ways to do this.

CHRISTIAN EDUCATION AND MULTIPLE INTELLIGENCE LEARNING

For decades there have been pockets of educators who were aware of the multiplicity of ways that we learn and wisely incorporated that knowledge into their classrooms. However, about twenty years ago, researchers began to take a broader look at the theories of intelligence, new brain research, and how we learn. Howard Gardner's book, *Frames of Mind: The Theory of Multiple Intelligences*, first published in 1983 and Robert Sylwester's book, *A Celebration of Neurons*, published in 1995, created some waves in public education. Continued research and classroom applications over the last twenty years in the theories of multiple intelligences and new brain research have changed the way many public educators view intelligence. Through the realization that there are many ways of learning, this research has also influenced significant changes in teaching methods.

The results of the studies suggested that most people learn using a variety of different intelligences—and each individual's strongest and weakest intelligences are unique to them. Most teaching has focused on verbal (linguistic) intelligence and mathematical (logical) intelligence. Learners whose primary intelligences are not those that are dominant in our culture are often considered less bright or labeled as troublemakers. Learners who learn best through musical (rhythmic) intelligence or body (kinesthetic) intelligence are often shamed for the inability to sit quietly and listen or do endless workbook and writing exercises to "catch up" with their classmates.

The transformations taking place in Christian education and the research on new brain theories had their beginnings in very different contexts and were motivated for very different reasons. Yet it seemed inevitable that the two would one day intersect.

With the 1996 publication of Barbara Bruce's book, *7 Ways of Teaching the Bible to Children*, multiple intelligence theories began to be taken seriously by Christian educators nation-wide. Gardner's theories provided a solid rationale for incorporating multiple intelligences into Christian education programs. The challenge for congregations has been to find new ways of teaching the age-old story by incorporating new methods that help to maximize all of the intelligences.

The groundwork laid by those first Christian educators who had unknowingly put the new research and theories into practice helped to bridge the gap—and the new theories helped to enhance and strengthen the work being done by pioneering Christian educators.

A MULTIPLE INTELLIGENCE APPROACH TO CREATIVE MUSIC

Howard Gardner has identified the following multiple intelligences. Each of the seven intelligences listed is accompanied by an example related to creative music.

➢ **Musical/Rhythmic:** Learners explore the many non-verbal sounds in the environment that are key to creative music. This exploration includes both traditional musical instruments and environmental sounds. Learners listen to, create, and play sounds to convey mood, character, and story line from biblical stories.

➢ **Logical/Mathematical:** Learners analyze the Bible story and the sounds around them to choose appropriate sounds to help convey the story. If a sound does not convey the right message, learners must first identify why it doesn't work and then seek a solution for a better sound.

➢ **Visual/Spatial:** Learners compose non-pitch specific compositions and write them down in chart or drawing form. The challenge is to "map" out a composition in such a way to allow others to follow it and perform the composition. The performers look at the chart or drawing and figure out what sounds or instruments should be played, and how and when they will be played. Compositions using traditional musical notation also require learners to use visual skills.

➢ **Verbal/Linguistic:** Learners create new lyrics for an existing melody to discover how to use language and words to tell a Bible story in a new way. Verbal skills are also used when critiquing compositions created by a group of learners and making suggestions for ways to change the composition to better convey the Bible story.

The challenge for congregations has been to find new ways of teaching the age-old story by incorporating new methods that help to maximize all of the intelligences.

➤ **Interpersonal:** Learners create new lyrics in a group setting to allow them to practice working as a team member and building consensus for the best words and phrases to use for the song. Performing a composition created by another learner requires cooperation and team effort. It also allows learners the opportunity to give positive feedback to the composer in a sensitive way.

➤ **Intrapersonal:** Learners create their own compositions or lyrics to allow one's feelings, interpretations, and strengths to emerge.

➤ **Bodily/Kinesthetic:** Learners move to music and perform musical compositions (vocal sounds and playing an instrument) to discover ways to use one's body to communicate.

Creative music is very much about actively doing something. It can easily involve aspects of all the seven intelligences. There will be some aspect in your creative music activities in which each learner can connect to his or her best learning styles. The more intelligences involved in each activity, the more learners will become engaged and positively affected by what happens.

Chapter 3

Exploring the Biblical Story

I like to use three main categories in approaching Bible stories when using creative music. Sounds and movement can explore the characters, the action of the story, and the mood in the story. Here are some examples.

CHARACTERS

In many stories we find at least one main character. After hearing the story, identify the characters in the story and determine who are the main ones and who played supporting roles. Focus on one character at a time and describe what he or she is like. Sample questions to ask include:

➤ How did she interact with other characters?

➤ How did he respond to what happened to him?

➤ How confident is she?

➤ Is he a likable person? Why or why not?

➤ What feelings did she express in the story?

➤ What kinds of things are important to him?

Include other questions as appropriate to the story.

Once you have a description of the character, you can begin to think of sounds that might communicate aspects of the character's personality. Try an exercise to get started. The chart on page 17 lists a variety of personality traits and behaviors. The second column gives a suggestion of a sound or combination of sounds to represent that trait or behavior. Write your ideas for additional sound suggestions in the third column.

Each character will most likely need several sounds played either in combination or in a sequence. Characters sometimes change during the course of a story. Take Zacchaeus, for example. His encounter with Jesus changed his life! It also changed other people's perceptions of Zacchaeus. Either the sounds representing Zacchaeus or the way the original sounds are played need to change during the course of the story.

Exploring characters through sound can be fun whether done simply or with some complexity. It also helps children learn ways to identify the feelings of others and ways to express their own feelings.

Exploring the Characters with Sound

Trait or Behavior	Sound Suggestions	Your Sound Suggestions
Timid	Softly tapping a pencil on the table. The tapping is uneven. Sometimes there are pauses between a series of taps.	
Angry	Loud pounding on a drum.	
Joyful	Shaking tambourine, set of keys, or other metallic tinkling sounds.	
Fearful	Moaning sounds while intermittently shaking a jar half full of buttons.	
Confident	Marching around the room while beating out a repeated rhythm pattern on sticks.	
Curious	Several sounds (such as paper rustling, vocal clicking, electric pencil sharpener and pencil) done in sequence over and over again, getting louder each time.	
Sad	Softly closing a door several times with a long period of silence between each closing.	
Gentle	Slow shuffle sound with feet accompanied by soft triangle sounds.	

ACTION

When you explore the characters in a story you connect with what is happening to them. Begin outlining the action in the story, putting the events in the order they happened. Then you're ready to select sounds to represent the action in the story. Let your imagination go. There is no need to come up with sounds that *exactly* match what's happening. This isn't an exercise in only creating sound effects for the story. Instead, you are trying to create images with sound.

God told Noah to build an ark. In response to that command, Noah worked on the ark, encountered his neighbors' reactions, gathered animals, and so forth. A lot of action occurred during this story. Children can have a wonderful time putting together sounds to help tell what's going on. Here are a few ideas to get your imagination going. (Refer to the sound chart on page 19.)

> *Building the ark.* You will probably want to include some pounding sound effects. But there must have been more to building an ark than pounding. Ask the children to explore the text and think about building an ark thousands of years ago. Noah wouldn't have had a local lumberyard to go to for his building materials. What would he and his family have to do to get this ark built?

> *Encounters with the neighbors.* Decide on a sound or sound combination to represent Noah and a very different sound or sound combination to represent the neighbors. Alternate the sounds to represent a conversation between Noah and the others. What was the tone of their conversation? What if we assume that there were conversations throughout the time the ark was being built? The result would be a sound composition that contains building sounds alternating with conversation sounds.

> *Gathering the animals.* Ask the children to choose about six animals that went into the ark. Choose a sound to represent each animal. Begin with playing the sound for the first animal. As it continues to play, add one sound at a time until all six sounds are playing together.

A similar layering effect, as done in the story with the animals, could be done with the creation story in Genesis. A different sound could be assigned for each day of creation. By the end of the story, all of the sounds of creation would be present together.

There are a variety of ways to "tell" the action for any given story. Each group of learners could come up with a different composition. Learners will be using musical elements such as fast and slow, loud and soft, long and short in their compositions. They will also learn how to organize sounds to get the desired effect. But this is more than a music lesson. It is an opportunity for children to experience, tell, and remember what happened in a particular Bible story. Have your learners perform the sound chart on page 19 or some of their own.

Exploring the Action with Sound

A sample chart for Noah's Ark story
xx=playing sound

Build ark	xx		xx		xx								
Talking		xx		xx		xx							
Animal 1							xx	xx	xx	xx	xx	xx	
Animal 2								xx	xx	xx	xx	xx	
Animal 3									xx	xx	xx	xx	
Animal 4										xx	xx	xx	
Animal 5											xx	xx	
Animal 6												xx	

MOOD

Some Bible stories project a definite mood. Depending on what happens throughout the story, the mood may change. Consider the first Passover in Egypt. Depending on your point of view (Israelite or Egyptian), you would describe one of two different moods.

This would be true at the Red Sea, too. Although first concerned for their safety, later Miriam and the other women were dancing with joy, praise, and thanksgiving to God.

Mood in a story can be explored through both sound and movement. Following are questions and directions to help learners delve into the mood of a story. Use the chart on page 21 to record your ideas.

➤ As a listener, what words would you use to describe the mood of the story you have chosen?

➤ Choose one of the main characters in the story. As that character, what words would you use to describe the mood of what's happening in the story?

➤ Were the words you used to describe the mood as a listener and as one of the characters the same or different? Why or why not?

➤ What sounds can you demonstrate (using instruments or found sounds) that help describe the mood in the story?

➤ Choose one of the words to describe the mood. Move your body as many different ways as you can to show that mood.

➤ What sounds and movements go together to describe the mood in the story?

➤ What sound and movement combinations best describe the mood?

Using sounds and movements to explore moods can also be helpful when stories are gathered into units. When themes run through several stories, sound and movement combinations can be used over and over again to provide some "glue" throughout the unit. Themes such as celebration, peace, and praise lend themselves well to sound and movement combinations. A new combination could be created for each story in the unit. By the end of the unit, a larger musical composition could be put together using the various combinations already developed.

When working with stories, the three categories of characters, action, and mood often overlap one another. That is fine. In each story, one of the categories will probably stand out the strongest. Let that guide you as you plan your learning activities. Begin with the category that is most accessible to children. Then use what you have available, add a little imagination, try a few samples, and have fun with the results!

Exploring the Mood with Sound

Describe the mood of the story from the listener's point of view.	
Sounds to describe that mood	
Body movement to show that mood	
Describe the mood of the story from the main character's point of view.	
Sounds to describe the main character's mood	
Body movements to show the main character's mood	

Chapter 4

Collecting Sounds and Instruments

I remember visiting a friend's cabin on a lake. The cabin was at the end of a lake where no other people were living. The cabin had no electricity or phone. One summer I was the first to arrive. I shut off my car engine and got out of the car. At first I noticed the silence. Then I gradually started to hear the sounds of the wildlife living around the cabin area. It was a treat to my ears to have something different to listen to.

TAPPING INTO SOUNDS

Have you ever thought about all of the potential sounds around you? There are probably quite a few sounds around you right now. What are you hearing? How many can you list? How many of them are generated by something electric? When the electrical power went out for a short time last week, I was reading the newspaper. I knew something had happened because there was a different kind of silence. All the humming from electrical motors had stopped. Once my ears and brain had adjusted to the fact that the quiet hum I usually tune out was missing, I started to notice other sounds.

But some of the things you hear are just noise, you say? Let's try to make a distinction between sounds and noise. I think of noise as the sounds that you don't have much control over and may not find particularly pleasant. The problem with classifying what is and what is not noise is that it can fluctuate a lot depending on the person and the mood he or she is in on a particular day. For example, children's voices playing outside on a playground might be considered happy sounds by one person and irritating noise by another.

Of the sounds you listed earlier, how many of them would you classify as noise and how many are sounds you would consider interesting or pleasant? How many sounds are ones that you can have some control over (such as unplugging the phone, turning off the radio, and so forth)?

The next thing to consider is how to use the interesting or pleasant sounds we can make. Even a sound that you may find interesting can become unpleasant under certain circumstances. For example, a toddler playing the piano keys and exploring the sounds it makes can be an important learning experience. When the toddler decides that only repeated banging (more times than you can count) on the piano will do, it is no longer music to your ears. So even though we are talking about using "environmental" sounds for instruments, we are still working with concepts of music.

IDENTIFYING POTENTIAL INSTRUMENTS

Here's an idea of some potential instruments you might have around your home.

➢ pencil

➢ book

➢ wastebasket

➢ coins

➢ keys

➢ plastic bag

➢ paper bag

➢ tissue paper

➢ soup can

➢ plastic soft drink bottle

➢ pots and pans

➢ newspaper

➢ wood blocks

➢ kitchen utensils (wooden spoons, spatulas, whisks, and so forth)

➢ dried leaves

➢ broom

➢ pail

➢ balloons

➢ hairbrush

➢ shoes

➢ string of beads

➢ chair

➢ table

➢ stool with rungs

➢ rubber band

➢ paper clip

➢ comb

This is a short list. What items would you add to it? Remember to keep safety in mind as you make your list (no power tools!). Do the same listing exercise as you look around your church building and your classroom space.

fast

loud

short

long

even

slow

low

high   **uneven**   **soft**

The next step is to stretch your imagination to think of as many different sounds for each item as possible. For example, how many different sounds can you get from newspaper? For starters, you can tear it, crumple it, flap it, and tap it with a pencil. How do the sounds you make with newspaper differ from those made with tissue paper?

Don't forget the sounds we can make with our bodies. We can:

➣ clap our hands

➣ snap our fingers

➣ tap our feet

➣ pat our thighs

➣ tap our cheeks

➣ pat our heads

➣ thump our elbows on the table

➣ drum our fingers on the table

Again, the list could go on and on. We can also make sounds with our mouths and voices. We can:

➣ click our tongues

➣ whistle (well, some of us can!)

➣ hum

➣ murmur

➣ smack our lips

Children will have a wonderful time adding to these two lists!

SAMPLE EXERCISES

Following are sample exercises to do with learners to stretch their imaginations when listening for the sounds around them.

Exercise 1

Give each learner a copy of "Find the Sounds in This Room" found on page 26. Ask them to list all the items in the picture with which they could make at least one sound. Compare lists when everyone is finished. (Have younger learners say the name of the item out loud and make a list on newsprint or board for everyone to see.) Ask the learners how they would make a sound with the items on their list.

Exercise 2

Give each learner a piece of paper and a pencil. Take them on a tour of the church building. Ask them to write or draw a picture of at least four objects they see that could be used to make sounds.

Exercise 3

Give each learner a copy of "Making Sounds with Objects" on page 27. Collect one or more samples of each of the objects so the learners can experience making sounds with them. Ask learners to come up with as many sounds as they can for each object. Second, ask learners to choose one sound for each item. Invite them to combine the sounds of two or more items and play them at the same time. What sound combinations do they like best?

Find the Sounds in This Room!

_____   _____

_____   _____

_____   _____

_____   _____

_____   _____

Making Sounds with Objects

Object	Sounds to Make
Empty plastic soft drink bottle	
Key ring with several keys on it	
Tissue paper	
Hairbrush	
String of beads	

COLLECTING INSTRUMENTS

Collecting environmental sounds for use as instruments should be fun and fairly easy. It is also important to collect traditional instruments to have available as you and your learners seek to create music in conjunction with Bible stories. The two types of instruments (environmental and traditional) can work together in helping learners create just the right type of sound they want for their compositions. For example, the sound of flapping cloth or paper might be exactly what your learners want. Another sound they want might best be accomplished by striking and shaking a tambourine.

Traditional rhythm instruments are one category of instruments very useful in working with creative music. Your congregation may already have some of these and other types of instruments available to you. If not, some can be made or purchased for use in creative music learning sessions. Following are a few tips to get you started.

➤ Look around your building and talk with any choir directors and music leaders. There may already be instruments that you can use.

➤ If instruments need to be obtained, check on the budget for education programs to see if some instruments or materials to make some instruments can be purchased.

➤ If instruments are to be purchased, be sure to get quality instruments. Beware of some of the children's rhythm band instrument sets found in toy stores. For quality of sound and durability, check carefully the quality of the products you purchase.

➤ If instruments are to be made, see the instructions on page 29.

Once you have determined what's already available and what resources you have for obtaining additional instruments, you can think about the specific instruments you need for your sessions. Budgets are rarely unlimited, so it is a good idea to prioritize which instruments are most essential. Following is one suggestion for getting started.

Key Items	Good to Have
hand drum (comfortable for children)	cymbals
tambourine	tone bells or xylophone
keyboard	wood block
triangle	guitar
rhythm sticks	jingle bells
maracas	sand blocks

However you prioritize your list, be sure to include instruments that shake, produce high and low pitched sounds, provide sustained sounds, provide sharp or short sounds, and can be played by children.

Other instruments can be added to your list as you identify instruments learners play. As children get older, some will choose to learn how to play musical instruments. If you want a plucked sound, ask someone who plays a string instrument to bring it in for a session. Tap into the many resources that learners can contribute to each session.

MAKING INSTRUMENTS

Making your own instruments can be both fun and cost effective. Some instruments can be made by children. If you plan for all of the children to make the same instrument, they can choose to take them home to use.

Here are some basic suggestions for making instruments.

Rhythm Sticks

Materials: thick dowels, saw, sandpaper
Instructions: Cut dowels into 8" (20 cm) or 12" (30 cm) lengths. Smooth ends with sandpaper.

Triangle

Materials: wire hanger, string, metal stick
Instructions: Attach a piece of string to a wire hanger. The string should be long enough so that it loops over the palm of your hand. Hold the hanger by the string and strike the hanger with a metal stick.

Horn

Materials: empty gallon or half-gallon plastic milk jug, scissors
Instructions: Cut off the bottom of the plastic jug. Sing, hum, or blow through the small opening.

Collecting Sounds and Instruments

Maracas

Materials: small empty containers with lids (large baby food jars, jelly jars, and so forth), small objects (beads, aquarium rocks, and so forth)

Instructions: Place small objects in container until half full. Secure top. Shake to see if you get the sound you want. Adjust amount of small objects accordingly. Glue or securely tape lid on to keep the lid from coming loose. Shake.

Shaker

Materials: stapler, crayons, markers, crepe paper streamers (optional), small objects (beads, aquarium rocks, and so forth), sturdy paper plates (two for each shaker)

Instructions: Pour small objects on a paper plate. Place a second paper plate over it so that rims touch. Staple all the way around the edges of the two plates, stapling close enough together so that none of the objects can leak out. Decorate plates with crayons, markers, and with short crepe paper streamers. Shake and tap.

Jingle Bells

Materials: jingle bells, thread, 12" (30 cm) lengths of sturdy ribbon or cording

Instructions: Sew several jingle bells, evenly spaced, onto a sturdy 12" (30 cm) piece of ribbon or cording. Make certain the bell is sewn loosely enough so that it can ring freely when shaken. Securely sew or tie ends together to make a circle. Shake.

Cymbals

Materials: drawer pulls or small pieces of wood, metal pie tins, nail, screws, screwdriver

Instructions: Use the nail to poke a hole through the center of the pie tin. Securely attach one drawer pull or wood with a screw to each metal pie tin. The drawer pull or wood serves as a handle. Clash two pie tins together.

Harp

Materials: wood or heavy cardboard, saw, variety of lengths and thicknesses of rubber bands

Instructions: Cut a rectangle from the wood or cardboard. Cut out the center of the rectangle. Make slits on the outside for the rubber bands. Place different sized rubber bands in the slits. Pluck the rubber bands.

Sand Blocks

Materials: 3" x 2" x 1" (8 cm x 5 cm x 2 cm) blocks of wood, wood glue, drawer pulls, sandpaper, staples

Instructions: Glue or staple a 3" x 3" (8 cm x 8 cm) piece of sandpaper to the 3" (8 cm) side of the block of wood. Overlap ½" (1 cm) of sandpaper on each side of the 2" (5 cm) side of the block of wood. (As an alternative, you could staple the sandpaper to the wooden block.) Rub the blocks together. On the opposite side of the block, glue drawer pulls.

Chapter 5

Preparing Leaders

NO TUNE-CARRYING BUCKETS NEEDED

How many times have you heard someone say one of the following?

I can't tell the difference between a horn and a fiddle. I haven't got a clue about music.

I don't know anything about music. I can't even play Chopsticks on the piano.

I can't carry a tune in a bucket. I don't even sound good in the shower!

I have no sense of rhythm.

When someone learns I have taught music, it is not unusual for me to get two basic responses. One is a bit of fear, although I don't consider myself an intimidating person. People make comments like those above and immediately disqualify themselves from any musical activity I might have in mind for them. Do they think that I am going to burst into song right there on the spot and ask everyone to join me? Or perhaps they think I will whip out a tambourine from my purse and test their rhythm in front of everyone? If I said I was a golf instructor, would they expect me to have a golf club with me and ask them to show me their golf swing? I don't go around conducting music classes in church hallways after worship services. Leaders and teachers in creative music learning sessions will not be asked to do that either.

32 Creative Music, Kids, and Christian Education

The second response I get starts with a gleam in their eyes. Perhaps they think a music educator will take care of all the music needs in the congregation's programs for children and they won't have to get involved. It's true that not everyone will want to lead creative music activities with children. We all have different interests. What saddens me is when someone who loves music doesn't feel able to lead creative music learning activities because he or she can't carry a tune.

You don't have to be a great singer or be the best pianist to lead creative music learning activities. Use the following checklist to see if you have potential as a creative music activity leader. Try it out with others in your congregation to see who might be interested in leading creative music, too.

Yes	No	Statement
❑	❑	I like music.
❑	❑	I like different kinds of music
❑	❑	(jazz, folk, classical, gospel, rock, and so forth).
❑	❑	I like experimenting with different kinds of sounds.
❑	❑	I like to try new things.
❑	❑	I have a good imagination.
❑	❑	I like to play with words.
❑	❑	I can tell the difference between long sounds and short sounds.
❑	❑	I can tell when sounds are fast or slow.
❑	❑	I can tell the difference between high sounds and low sounds.
❑	❑	I can tell when sounds are loud or soft.

If you answered yes to a number of these statements, then you have the potential and skills to work with creative music. Plus, you don't need to carry that bucket with you anymore!

TAPPING INTO MUSIC RESOURCES

Were you surprised at how many of the statements you were able to check "yes"? Music is an important part of so many cultures. It is an important part of how humans express their deepest feelings. Even for those who have had limited musical training or do not feel particularly gifted musically, music is part of life. It is something we can feel connected to regardless of our skill level.

Tapping What's inside Yourself

You have resources inside yourself that can be of value to children in creative music learning activities. What resources, you ask? Some will be easy to identify and others may take a little digging. Consider the following questions.

➢ What's your best childhood memory of something musical? Why was it the best?

➢ What musical activity do you enjoy the most these days? (Remember, it can be something like humming to yourself while you mow the lawn, tapping your fingers on the steering wheel to a song on the radio while you wait at a red light, listening to a favorite CD, and so forth.) Why is it your most enjoyable activity?

➢ What's one musical thing you've always wanted to do, but never had the opportunity or courage to do? (You can dream really big here if you want to!) Why have you always wanted to do this?

➢ What musical skills do you feel you do at least moderately well? (Remember, this can be anything—clapping your hands to the beat, listening actively at a concert, being an awesome drummer, or discovering new musical talent.) List as many as you can. Don't be modest!

➢ What type of creative music learning activity would you most like to try? Why does it interest you?

Perhaps these questions have started the wheels turning and you discovered more than you thought would be there. Think about what you have enjoyed, in both the past and present, and how that might be an asset to the children in your church. Remember to focus on what you can do and enjoy, rather than on what you can't do.

Music is an important part of so many cultures. It is an important part of how humans express their deepest feelings.

Tapping into What Others Have to Offer

There are a variety of ways to assess the musical resources others have to offer. Try some of the following:

➤ Make a list of the known musicians in your congregation. What specific skills do you know they have? Add those skills to your list.

➤ If other leaders and teachers did the same "tapping what's inside yourself" exercise above, share your results. There may be complementary interests and skills that can be exchanged depending on the stories you are exploring with the learners.

➤ Check with known musicians about other musical interests and skills they have that have not been tapped by the congregation yet.

➤ Explore with others you know in the congregation what their untapped musical interests and skills might be. Survey them with the five questions listed on page 34. What are the results? Are there specific things you want to make note of for future reference? How willing might they be to assist you with an activity?

Remember that not all musicians are comfortable with creative music activities that use environmental sounds. When asking for assistance on something, you may need to brief them on what you are planning to do and why. One option might be to lead a session with a group as a demonstration of what creative music learning activities are all about.

God has given us the gift of music and a variety of gifts and talents in ourselves. Our task is to look around us and identify and use the resources we have been given.

GETTING READY

In the previous chapters we've been setting the stage for preparing and leading creative music learning activities. Now is the time to be specific. Use the questions and suggestions from the worksheet "Leading Creative Music" on pages 36-37 to help you prepare to lead in your setting.

Leading Creative Music

1. How many learners are in your group? Consider what would and would not work well with that size group. What modifications would need to be made for different types of activities? Groups of two to three may need to combine with another group if you anticipate creating a sound composition incorporating five or six sounds, for example.

2. What are the ages of the learners in your group? How broad a range do you have?

3. What skills do the learners already have?

➤ Can they keep a steady beat? If they can't, you may want to narrow the focus of your session and spend some time learning to do this better. Eye contact between learners and leaders is the key to keeping a steady beat!

➤ Do they enjoy playing with words? If so, you might create new words to tell the Bible story using a well-known melody.

➤ Are they able to read a chart? (See page 62 for sample of a chart.) Charting a sound composition often works well with older learners. Younger learners often require a leader to signal to them when it is time for them play and when it is time to stop.

➤ Find out what musical things your learners like to do and where they have some competency. Older children may be learning to play an instrument and would enjoy having the opportunity to play in a class activity—especially if they get to make an unconventional sound with it.

4. It is very important that all learners participate actively in the session. Creative music learning activities are very conducive to getting everyone involved. Again, consider your learners. Would some make good directors? Is there a sound or instrument for everyone to play? If not, reinforce sharing!

5. Giving a group of children instruments or environmental sounds can be chaotic and noisy if you don't have some guidelines in place before you begin. Guidelines could include such things as:

> ➤ play your instrument or sound only when directed

> ➤ listen to the sounds other learners are making

> ➤ stop playing your instrument or sound when a predetermined signal is given

Additional guidelines could incorporate such issues as caring for the instruments and cleaning up once the session is over. Create a list of guidelines for your group. Share them with the learners, asking them to offer suggestions for additional guidelines or modifications to your list.

6. Remember that creative music learning activities focus on the process, not a polished performance. Allow children the opportunity to try their creations several times. Ask for suggestions on what they think should be added, deleted, or modified to make it sound better.

7. Remember that creative music learning activities are not equivalent to chaotic noise. Creativity has structure. Music has structure. The balance between "do anything you want" and a rigid "it can only be done this way" is key. Review some of the basic concepts of music on page 6. Use those concepts to help shape what you do with sound. There is a lot of freedom within those concepts, and yet they will help you and your learners create something that has some meaning.

Chapter 6

Setting Up the Music Learning Environment

Where your sessions take place and the types of materials you have available for use can be just as important as the activities planned for the session. This chapter will suggest ways to make the learning environment and all that is contained in it the best possible place for creative music activities to happen.

MATERIALS

Use the following list to help gather the materials you will need to lead creative music sessions. Remember that different types of activities will require different kinds of materials. You will not need everything for every session.

- ➤ paper
- ➤ pencils
- ➤ markers
- ➤ tape player
- ➤ blank tapes to record your group's compositions
- ➤ variety of music recordings
- ➤ CD player
- ➤ Firelight Creative Music CD
- ➤ chalkboard or whiteboard

(Note: A large writing surface, visible to everyone, is needed in order to chart out compositions created by the group. (See pages 62-64 for examples of compositions.) If you do not have a large board, then taping several sheets of newsprint together and attaching them to the wall would also work.)

- ➤ chalk or dry-erase markers
- ➤ newsprint and easel
- ➤ collection of "found" sounds (newspapers, keys, kitchen utensils, and so forth)—see page 23
- ➤ songbooks with traditional children's songs (see chapter 8)
- ➤ songbooks with Christian songs and hymns for children

➤ variety of instruments (drum, tambourine, guitar, piano, and so forth)
List the instruments available to you here:

➤ homemade instruments (see page 29)
List the instruments available to you here:

There may be additional materials needed for a specific session. The above list is a general list of materials that may be used through a series of sessions.

SPACE NEEDS

The amount of space needed depends on the type of activity the group will be doing. Activities that direct learners to move to music will require more space than activities involving learners in creating new lyrics to a well-known melody. Following are general suggestions to help plan space needs for a variety of creative music learning activities. Understand that these suggestions are for the ideal situation and are not always possible for every school or congregation.

Moving to music

> area free of furniture or other obstacles

> large, tacked-down carpet to prevent slips and falls

> large enough space so that all learners can be involved in movement activities at the same time

Making instruments

> room with tables and chairs

> place for instruments to be set if paint or glue needs to dry

Creating new lyrics

> space with chalkboard, whiteboard, or newsprint on an easel

Creating and performing sound compositions

> space with chalkboard, whiteboard, or large wall on which to tape multiple sheets of newsprint

> space for a variety of instruments and found sounds

> "elbow room" for each learner to play his or her instrument or sound

STORING INSTRUMENTS AND SOUNDS

It is important to have the materials needed for creative music learning activities ready and available for teachers and leaders of all ages in your Christian education program. One ideal situation would be to have a good-sized room designated as the creative music learning room and any teacher who planned to use creative music learning as a primary focus of a session would schedule to use the room. All of the materials listed earlier in this chapter would be stored in that room.

Since many of us do not have that ideal option available to us, I will suggest another option: try making a creative music cart. The cart would contain all of the smaller materials listed above. It could be moved to whichever room or space best suited the type of activity planned. Since many congregations have rooms of different shapes and sizes for their education programs, not all rooms may be

appropriate for creative music learning activities. The movable cart option would also require some flexibility on the part of leaders to switch rooms to accommodate groups doing different activities on any given day.

The cart needs several shelves. Gather several large plastic boxes with covers. Use the boxes to store purchased instruments, homemade instruments, "found sound" examples, audio equipment, songbooks, and paper and marker supplies. Items too large for the cart will need to be gathered separately. Large congregations may need to put together more than one cart.

"DO NOT DISTURB"

One of the challenges of doing some of the types of creative music learning activities described in this book is finding a place that will not disturb other groups of learners. Let's face it—the majority of creative music learning activities are not going to be quiet. We're focused on sounds and how they can be used to express stories, characters, and feelings.

Finding the best space possible in your facility is critical to the willingness of everyone in your Christian education program to include creative music as a part of the program. If your group is sharing a room with another group and all you have is a portable room divider between you, then some of the activities will require you to temporarily find another space. If your group is dancing, singing, and playing tambourines during the "Song of Miriam" session or the sound composition of the story of the good Samaritan gets loud as the traveler is getting robbed, then a space away from other groups of learners is needed. No matter how wonderful the session is to your group, if sound levels are perceived as disturbing by others near your space, negative attitudes have a chance to develop and will hinder the potential for further activities of this nature.

Not all creative music learning activities are louder or more disturbing than other kinds of activities. But for the ones that can be loud, you need to consider what other groups are close by and how much they will hear. This is another example of how creative music learning activities require some flexibility. Groups may need to move around from session to session.

Consider the space set aside for learning programs in your facility.

➤ How many spaces for groups have full walls (not partitions) and doors?

➤ Are there any rooms that have only one group using them?

➤ Are outdoor spaces an option?

➤ Are there spaces not being used that could be used for an occasional creative music learning activity?

Answers to these questions will help determine where creative music learning activities can best occur. Finding a workable space allows everyone to focus on the activity without worrying about being too loud. A willingness of leaders to work together to arrange appropriate space(s) can enhance the learning environment and the goals for the session can be met.

Chapter 7

Session Helps

This chapter is for the leader who has decided to include creative music learning activities into sessions, has gathered the materials and music resources, found an appropriate place to do the activities, and now wants to plan out some sessions. The chapter includes suggestions for:

> expanding an existing session to include creative music learning activities where none already exist

> facilitating the creation of a sound composition

> charting sound compositions

> creating a new piece of music or writing new lyrics to an existing tune

Note: Firelight Bible Learning Curriculum provides additional audio resources that can be used to implement creative music. See "Using Firelight Resources for Creative Music" in Appendix A.

EXPANDING AN EXISTING SESSION

Not all curriculum resources include creative music learning activities in their session plans. This means that the leader needs to add to the plan or substitute creative music learning activities for other suggested activities. In either case, the leader is creating something new. Following are suggestions on how to create your own plan.

> Consider the Bible texts for the sessions you are to teach. Some texts will lend themselves more easily to creative music learning activities than other texts. If you are just getting started with these types of activities, choose texts in which ideas flow more freely for you.

> Once you've chosen a text, go back and review chapter 3. Consider the characters, the action in the story, and the mood of the story. If you had to choose between characters, action, and mood, which category seems strongest to you in your chosen text?

> Begin by focusing on the strongest category. What kinds of sounds come to mind when you think of that category along with the story in the text?

> Consider how those sounds can be organized. How can they be used to help tell or experience the story?

➤ Present the text to learners. Ask them questions that explore the characters, action, and mood of the story. Which category do they think is the strongest? Is it the same category as you chose? If not, do they have a good point? If so, you can make some on-the-spot modifications to your plan.

➤ Plan for ways that the learners can choose sounds. Plan for ways the learners can organize the sounds.

Following are plans for two different Bible stories. They will help you see how creative music learning activities can flow out of a story.

The Creation Story

The first example is the creation story from Genesis 1-2:4. The action of God's creating the heavens and the earth and all living things is very strong. Thus, the action category is the strongest to use. It's a great opportunity to focus on the power of God's creative act.

The first thing to do with learners is to focus on the different things God created on each day. The key to doing any creative music learning activity focused on a Bible text or story is that the learners know the text.

First make a list of what happened on each day, and then match sounds to each day of creation. Also list what kinds of body movements might be appropriate for each day. This text lends itself well to combining sound and movement. This step of the process is complete when (1) there is a sound or combination of sounds for each day of creation, and (2) there are body movements to use for each day of creation. To help everyone remember the choices, make a simple chart like the one on page 63. The chart can use words or pictures.

The text provides a separation between each day. Choose a sound that signals to the learners when the sounds and movement for one day start and stop. One option is to include a narrator who reads the text, divided by days between the sounds and movement segments. The sound signal is given after the text segment is read and before the next segment begins. Including the text being read allows learners to put down one instrument and pick up another instrument between sound segments.

Try the entire piece. Evaluate with the learners what they heard and experienced. Did the sounds chosen for each day "say" what they wanted to express? If not, take some time to discuss what changes they would like to try. Regardless of whether or not changes were made, try the piece again. If it works really well, the group may wish to try it without the full text, limiting the narrator to naming each day (such as "The first day" and so forth).

Once the group has the composition the way they like it, consider recording it. The recording could also be used to provide the music for the movement activities used to tell the story.

The Plagues in Egypt

This example describes the ten plagues that occurred before the Pharaoh allowed Moses and the Hebrews to leave Egypt. The first plague begins in Exodus 7:14 and the tenth plague concludes at Exodus 12:32.

One activity for this story is to write new lyrics set to an existing melody to tell the story. (See pages 52-54 for suggestions of well-known melodies.) It would have at least 11 verses, one to set the stage and one for each plague. Choose an existing melody that has a refrain. Use the refrain to tell of Pharaoh's refusal to let the people go since this is a recurring section throughout the story.

Because the story is long, creating new lyrics to an existing melody would work best with older learners. Start with the refrain. Consider creating a few verses over several sessions. Unless the creative juices are flowing fast and furiously, trying to create 11 verses in one session will most likely lead to frustration if you don't run out of time first. Gauge how many verses your group can write by their participation and energy level. Once completed, they will have a great time singing their version of the plagues!

FACILITATING THE CREATION OF A SOUND COMPOSITION

Congratulations! If you are reading this section of the book, then you have either decided to try creating sound compositions with your group or are at least seriously considering it. If you have never done one before, have a great time helping your learners shape a composition they can call their own.

Facilitating a group as they create a sound composition is really a process of asking questions and then helping them mold their answers and choices into the shape they want. The facilitator needs some group consensus building skills, since not everyone will want the same sounds or instruments for a particular part of a composition. I have found that if everyone feels they have contributed something specific to the creation of the composition, they are usually satisfied. Older learners can create their own individual compositions once they get the hang of the process.

The chart on the next page contains general steps for the process where the text has a strong character component. The chart also contains how the steps work using a specific story, in this case the good Samaritan. Adapt as appropriate to the Bible text used in the session, especially if the text has strong action or mood components.

Steps in Process	Sample Story: The Good Samaritan
Ask learners: Who is in this story?	Man traveling to Jericho, robbers, priest, temple helper, man from Samaria
Who are the main characters? (identifying characters)	Man from Samaria, priest, and temple helper (i.e. the neighbors)
Ask learners: What do the characters do in this story? (identifying action)	The man walks on a journey. Robbers beat the man and leave. The priest and temple helper walk on past the man. The man from Samaria stops and helps the man, taking him somewhere to be taken care of.
Ask learners: How do you think the characters felt about what happened or what they did? How does the story make you feel? (identifying mood)	Feelings include: fear, power, greed, pity, caring
Once learners know the story, it's time to start matching sounds with characters, action, and mood. Begin with the characters. Some characters may need just one sound, while others would be best represented by several sounds. Try out sounds to make sure the sounds chosen match the types of characters and their feelings.	*Man:* tambourine *Robbers:* stomping feet *Priest:* maracas *Temple helper:* waving paper *Man from Samaria:* triangle
How will the sound be played to best portray the action of the character? Consider music concepts of fast/slow, loud/soft, high/low, long/short. Ask learners making each sound to practice their sound, "playing" the sound variations needed for the composition.	*Man:* steady tapping as he walks along road fast and loud shaking as robbers attack him *Robbers:* quiet, steady stamping of feet as they approach the man; loud, fast stamping as they attack the man; stamping gets softer and eventually stops as the robbers run away *Priest:* soft, steady maracas as priest enters the story; gets louder as he approaches the man; a few pauses in between sounds as he sees man; gets softer as he continues on his way *Temple helper:* similar sequence as the priest *Man from Samaria:* soft, long sounds on the triangle as he approaches the man
Choose a symbol to represent each sound.	See symbols on chart on page 62.

CHARTING SOUND COMPOSITIONS

Without using notes or other notation, you can write down the sounds learners have chosen, put them in the desired sequence, and perform the composition from your chart. Because you are not using words, even young children can follow along. Depending upon how you time your composition, someone will probably need to cue sounds when they are to begin and when they are to stop.

On pages 62-64 there are several sample charts containing sound compositions. The first one is for the story of the good Samaritan outlined on page 45.

Using the Charts

These charts are samples of one way to chart out a sound composition. Symbols for each sound can be as simple or as elaborate as you want. Be creative! Or better yet, let the group decide what symbol should be drawn for each sound. The important thing is that the performers of the sounds know when to play.

The chart for the story of the good Samaritan includes the sounds chosen earlier in this chapter. The symbols chosen vary in size to show the difference in when to play the sound loud or soft.

The charts for the creation story and "Jesus, Our Vine" have not designated a specific sound or instrument for each part. They are samples of one way the sounds could be arranged. There are no designations for the music concepts of fast/slow, loud/soft, long/short, high/low, and so forth. The learners can discuss more details as the composition takes shape. They can also add suggestions for how to represent the musical concept changes that need to happen in order for the composition to best represent the story. Help learners to understand that by using the music concepts, they will have a much more interesting and pleasing result. A composition that consists of several sounds played the same way, especially loud, all the way through is not interesting or pleasing, and probably will not convey the characters, action, and/or mood desired.

CREATING A NEW PIECE OF MUSIC OR WRITING NEW LYRICS

It can be a lot of fun to create a new musical piece, especially one that tells the story of God working in the lives of people. There are several ways to do this with a group of children. One way is to create both a new melody and new words to form a new song. Another way to create a song about a Bible text is to write new words to an existing, familiar tune.

If you choose the first way, you will need a leader who can elicit phrases of melody from children, remember them, and write them down in traditional musical notation. This process does take more time because it involves helping learners create both melody (with rhythm) and lyrics. If you have a resource person in your congregation who can facilitate this process, it is a worthwhile activity to undertake. The end product is a song that the children truly feel is theirs. Having it written down in a form that others can read means that it will not be lost and thus has lasting value.

The second way, using an existing melody as a foundation for new words, has been done repeatedly over the centuries. Once an appropriate tune has been chosen, the group creating new words can concentrate on finding the words that best tell the story and fit the phrases and rhythm of the tune. The end product is a song that they created and that many others can quickly join them in singing.

Here, we'll focus on how to facilitate a group as they create new words for an existing melody. Keep in mind that the steps outlined below are general and may need to be adapted to fit your setting.

Prior to the session:

1. Study the Bible text for the session. Ask yourself questions about the characters, action, and mood.

2. Does one character stand out? Can you imagine the song being mainly about that one character? (Zacchaeus or Esther, for example?)

3. Is there a definite progression to the story? Should the main focus be from the perspective of what happened? (The stories of Noah or the first Passover, for example?)

4. Is there a definite mood to the story? This will help determine what kind of existing melody you want to choose. A tune for a story of celebration might be different from a tune reflecting a story about the Lord's Prayer, for example.

5. Consider how the characters, action, and mood blend together. Even though one category may emerge as strongest in a particular story, the other two categories will be present in the song.

6. Now begin thinking about existing melodies. See the list on pages 51-53 of both secular and sacred songs.

7. What melodies might your learners already know? Using a familiar melody saves time in the process and provides a solid musical base.

8. What kind of song structure would work best with the story? A story that will need lots of verses to tell it would benefit from a song that has a refrain.

9. What mood are you looking for? It's best not to choose a song with a mood and tempo that's quite different from the mood of the story. For example, you probably wouldn't want to choose "Zip-A-Dee Doo-Dah" for the melody to tell the story of the widow's penny or the first Passover.

10. Pick several melodies that you feel might work. This allows you to give your learners a few to choose from.

During the session:

1. Review the story with the learners.

2. Ask them about the characters, actions, and mood of the story.

3. Ask them to help you list key words or phrases from the story. This is especially helpful if the story is long. Be sure to include these key words or phrases in the song. Some examples might be:

> ➤ "It was good, and God said" (creation in Genesis 1)

> ➤ "vine, branches, and fruit" (John 15)

> ➤ "lamb and blood" (the first Passover in Exodus 12)

> ➤ "listening and worried" (Mary and Martha in Luke 10)

4. Ask them to help you list what should be included in the song in order to tell the story. This is especially helpful if the story is long.

5. If there is to be a refrain, determine what should be in the refrain.

6. Suggest the tunes to use for your new words you selected in your preparation time. Ask the group to choose one tune.

7. If there is a refrain, start by writing the words for that first.

8. When writing the words, don't feel that the last word in each line needs to rhyme. If rhyming works out, that's great. But not all songs have rhyming schemes. Don't let problems with trying to get things to rhyme block the creation of your song.

9. Start writing. Allow the children to brainstorm phrases. Help them match the number of syllables in the phrase of words to the number of notes in each phrase of the music. It's very difficult to sing a song that has too many words crammed into each phrase. If there are many more syllables than notes, try dividing the phrase in two and use with two lines of music.

10. Expect to do a lot of editing as a group during this process. It is not unusual for learners to make revisions that help the words better fit the melody and tell the story more clearly.

11. Once you have your first verse and/or refrain, sing it together to see how it works. When it feels right to the group, continue on with more verses as needed.

12. When completed to the group's satisfaction, sing it through several times. Also think about ways to share it with other groups. It might be a valuable and fun teaching tool for another group of learners. If you think your group will create several songs like this over the months, consider putting the songs together in a folder to create your own songbook.

13. Some songs will lend themselves well to adding movement or instruments. Add as appropriate.

Chapter 8

Resources

In previous chapters we have talked about a variety of resources. Some are the gifts within us and other people. Others involve the gathering and making of instruments and materials. Even the physical spaces in which we lead sessions and the discovery of sounds around us are resources for creative music learning activities.

GOING ON A TREASURE HUNT

This chapter focuses on helping you find and use song material for creative music learning activities. There may be abundant treasures around you just waiting to be discovered. Check out the following suggestions as you seek to complete the resource treasure-gathering you began in earlier chapters.

Look in storage areas in your congregation. If your congregation has been in its present building for at least a couple of decades, then there is a good chance you'll find something useful. Creative music learning activities don't require all new resources. Here's what to look for:

➢ Sunday school songbooks
➢ Hymnals
➢ Songbooks with traditional/well-known songs
➢ Recordings (choir or organ music, children's songs, instrumental music—both sacred and secular, and so forth)
➢ Anything else that looks interesting that you haven't already gathered as you read previous chapters

Talk with musicians in your congregation. Children's choir directors, music leaders, and other musicians may have some music resources for you. The score from a children's musical about Jonah might have just the song in it that you need for a session you're planning. Ask musicians to tap their brains and their files and shelves for music resources. Types of things to look for include:

➢ children's choir pieces that are about a particular Bible story or character
➢ songs with motion
➢ rhythmic speech resources
➢ resources about using instruments with children

Any of these might provide material or ideas for a creative music learning session.

Check your storage areas at home. Do you have a favorite music book or recording from when you were a child or that you have used with children you know? Dig around and see what you can find.

Look for recordings of instrumental and environmental music. These can provide material for movement and mood. Shorter selections or short segments of longer selections work best with children. Types to look for:

➢ folk tunes and dances
➢ classical compositions
➢ overtures from musicals
➢ contemporary instrumental artists
➢ environmental recordings (whales, rainstorms, birds singing, and so forth)

Add more to the list here:

FAVORITE TRADITIONAL SONGS

Following is a sample list of songs that have been a part of traditional children's song repertoire over the decades. This is not meant to be an exhaustive list. It is instead designed to give you an idea of what types of songs to look for as you go on your treasure hunt.

➢ A Sailor Went to Sea
➢ A-Tisket, A-Tasket
➢ Alphabet Song
➢ The Animal Fair
➢ Are You Sleeping?
➢ Baa, Baa, Black Sheep
➢ Clementine
➢ Comin' thru the Rye
➢ Down by the Station
➢ Eentsy Weentsy Spider
➢ The Farmer in the Dell
➢ Going to the Zoo
➢ Head and Shoulders
➢ Hey, Lolly, Lolly
➢ Hickory Dickory Dock
➢ The Hokey-Pokey
➢ Home on the Range
➢ I Love the Mountains

- I Know an Old Lady
- If You're Happy
- I'm a Little Teapot
- The Inchworm
- Jimmy Crack Corn
- Lazy Mary
- London Bridge
- Looby-Loo
- Mary Had a Little Lamb
- The More We Get Together (Did You Ever See a Lassie?)
- The Muffin Man
- The Mulberry Bush
- O Susanna
- Oats, Peas, Beans
- Oh Where, Oh Where Has My Little Dog Gone?
- Old MacDonald Had a Farm
- On Top of Spaghetti
- Polly Wolly Doodle
- Pop! Goes the Weasel
- Reuben and Rachel
- Row, Row, Row Your Boat
- She'll Be Comin' Round the Mountain
- Shoo Fly
- Skip to My Lou
- This Old Man
- This Land Is Your Land
- Three Blind Mice
- Today Is Monday
- Twinkle, Twinkle, Little Star
- Waltzing Matilda
- Wheels on the Bus
- When the Saints Go Marching In
- Yankee Doodle

What additional songs do your learners know? List them here:

What additional songs do your learners know that are more current than the ones on the list? List them here:

FAVORITE SUNDAY SCHOOL SONGS

Following is a sample list of songs that have been a part of the children's Sunday school song repertoire over the decades. This is not meant to be an exhaustive list. It is instead designed to give you an idea of what types of songs to look for as you go on your treasure hunt. Some of the songs focus on a particular Bible story, while others have good melodies against which to set your own lyrics.

- A Mighty Fortress Is Our God
- All through the Night
- Child of God
- Children of the Heavenly Father
- The B-I-B-L-E
- Do Lord
- Down in My Heart
- Everybody Ought to Know
- Father Abraham
- Get On Board, Little Children
- Give Me Oil in My Lamp
- Hallelu, Hallelu
- Happy All the Time
- Heav'n, Heav'n (I Got a Robe)
- He's Got the Whole World
- His Banner over Me Is Love
- Jacob's Ladder
- Jesus Loves the Little Children
- Jesus Loves Me
- Joshua Fought the Battle of Jericho
- Little David, Play on Your Harp
- Oh, How I Love Jesus
- One More River
- Peace like a River
- Praise Him, Praise Him
- Rise and Shine
- Rock A' My Soul
- Seek Ye First
- Silver and Gold Have I None
- Standin' in the Need of Prayer
- Swing Low, Sweet Chariot
- This Little Light of Mine
- This Is the Day
- Who Built the Ark?
- Who Did Swallow Jonah?
- The Wise Man and Foolish Man
- Zacchaeus

What additional songs do your learners know? List them here:

What additional songs do your learners know that are more current than the ones on the list? List them here:

SONGBOOKS

Having a few songbooks at your fingertips can be very helpful when you need song material for your creative music learning activities. There are a number of songbook collections available in case you couldn't find any on your treasure hunt. The following songbooks can be obtained at local stores or through the Internet. Any of them can provide you with the tune and lyrics for a considerable number of songs. The list is just a sample of what's available.

Best Children's Songs Ever Songbook, Hal Leonard Publishing Corporation. ISBN 0-7935-8966-5

Big Book of Children's Songs, Hal Leonard Publishing Corporation. ISBN 0-7935-1357-X

Chatter with the Angels: An Illustrated Songbook for Children, Linda S. Richer and Anita Soltzfus Breckbill, editors, GIA Publications. ISBN 1-5799-9082-7

The Christian Children's Songbook: 101 Songs Kids Love to Sing, Hal Leonard Publishing Corporation, 2000. ISBN 0-6340-0336-4

The Definitive Children's Song Collection, Hal Leonard Publishing Corporation. ISBN 0-6430-0062-4

The Giant Book of Children's Songs, Cherry Lane Music. ISBN 0-8952-4821-2

Kids Classics Songbook, Volume 1, Cokesbury, 1993. ISBN 0-0050-0690-2

LifeSongs Songbook, Augsburg Fortress. ISBN 0-8066-4271-8 (available at www.augsburgfortress.org)

Singing the Story: Bible Songs of the Faithful, Kathy Tunseth. Augsburg Fortress. ISBN 0-8006-5443-9 (available at www.augsburgfortress.org)

Songs for Sunday School Music Book, Augsburg Fortress. ISBN 0-8066-3400-6 (available at www.augsburgfortress.org)

Wee Sing Songbook Series, Price Stern Sloan, Inc., Putnam & Grosset Group, New York. Some items in the series:

 Wee Sing America, CD/Cassette/Songbook
 Wee Sing and Play, CD/Cassette/Songbook
 Wee Sing Animals, Animals, Animals, Cassette/Songbook
 Wee Sing around the World, CD/Cassette/Songbook
 Wee Sing Bible Songs, CD/Cassette/Songbook
 Wee Sing Children's Songs and Fingerplays, CD/Cassette/Songbook
 Wee Sing Games Games Games, CD/Cassette/Songbook
 Wee Sing in the Car, Cassette/Songbook
 Wee Sing More Bible Songs, CD/Cassette/Songbook
 Wee Sing Nursery Rhymes and Lullabies, CD/Cassette/Songbook
 Wee Sing Silly Songs, CD/Cassette/Songbook
 Wee Sing Sing-Alongs, CD/Cassette/Songbook

Using Firelight Resources for Creative Music

USING THE FIRELIGHT CREATIVE MUSIC CD

The Creative Music CD includes sound effects, mood music, spoken word rhythms, and an example of a story composition. This recorded creative music can be used as a teaching tool or as a way to supplement the creative music that you compose.

This CD was originally produced to go with Firelight Bible Learning Curriculum for use by classroom teachers, Deeper Learning leaders, and leaders who sing with several groups of learners, but it can be used in any creative music program.

Here are examples of a variety of elements you can use to carry out creative music learning activities through movement and the creation of new music.

➤ samples of mood music to help learners understand how music can portray moods and feelings, some of which will match the characters they encounter in the Bible texts

➤ six original musical tracks that help set the mood of a story

➤ backbeats (rhythm tracks) for use as a foundation for short compositions created by learners

➤ sample of a sound composition using narration and sounds to tell a story

➤ sample of twenty sounds, including:
  - sounds of nature (rainstorm, night sounds, storm at sea, thunder, rushing wind, rushing water, fire crackling)
  - instrumental sounds (shofar, harp, bells)
  - coins jingling
  - Middle Eastern market place sounds
  - whip snapping
  - creaking door
  - wooden wheels on cobblestones
  - horse hooves
  - carpentry sounds
  - glass breaking
  - pouring water
  - forging metal

Mood Music

The CD contains a sampling of five compositions designed to evoke certain moods and emotions. A sixth composition is designed to evoke a sense of being transported to Bible times through the use of music with Middle Eastern elements in it. Following are ways to use the six tracks.

➤ Invite learners to identify the mood(s) from a particular Bible story. Play several of the tracks, asking learners to choose the one track that best matches the mood of the story.

➤ Choose a track that best matches the mood of a story. Invite learners to discuss what musical elements are present in the composition that help to convey the mood named in its title. What sounds or instruments would they choose to convey the same mood? After experimenting to find the right sounds, play the sounds or instruments with the track. Discuss how the combinations worked and what changes could be made to better convey the mood. Now create a new composition that conveys the same mood.

➤ Use one of the tracks as the foundation for a sound composition. Choose sounds and instruments to tell the story, creating a composition. Perform the composition while playing the track at the same time.

Sounds

The CD contains some wonderful sounds that can help learners experience a sampling of the sounds the characters in their Bible stories might have heard. The first seven tracks (shofar, Middle Eastern marketplace, snapping whip, wooden wheels on cobblestone streets, carpentry, forging metal, and horse hooves) are especially helpful for this. After listening to some or all of the seven tracks, ask learners the following types of questions:

➤ Which sounds might the characters in our Bible story have heard?

➤ What additional sounds might the characters have heard?

➤ How can we make some similar sounds using the objects and instruments we have here?

➤ What sound track(s) do we want to include in our composition for the story?

Sounds of nature are also included on the CD. Consider which ones connect with the stories you and the learners in your group are studying. Play any appropriate tracks and try the following suggestions:

➤ Create a sound composition related to one of the tracks, like a rainstorm, for example. Choose sounds and instruments that best convey the incident in nature. Consider using the sound composition as a part of a larger composition that tells the Bible story.

➤ Use one of the tracks as a foundation or an introduction for a composition telling the Bible story.

The remaining sounds can be used in a variety of ways in the music the learners create. A track might provide a recurring sound in their compositions, whether sung or with instruments. Coins jingling might occur in between each verse of a song about Zacchaeus, for example. The tracks might also inspire learners to record additional sound effects they want to include in compositions.

Share the Creative Music CD with leaders who are doing creative drama with learners. The sound effects may be useful for some of the activities they do with learners.

Spoken Word Rhythms

Three backbeats of different tempos are provided on the CD. Use these tracks to provide an instrumental foundation for spoken word or rap compositions. Match the track most appropriate to the mood of the story as you create this kind of composition.

Storytelling

The last track on the CD tells the story of the good Samaritan. It combines a sound composition representing the various characters of the story and the narration of the story. The chart of the sound composition can be found on page 62. Listen to the track with and without the sound composition chart. Try reading the story as learners play the sounds on the chart. With older learners especially, try performing the sound composition without the narration. Invite them to imagine the events of the story as the composition is played.

Allow your learners to suggest even more ways the CD can be used to enhance their exploration of God's word.

Firelight Creative Music CD
ISBN 0-8066-6446-0
(available at www.augsburgfortress.org)

USING THE FIRELIGHT SONG CDS

Additional resources are the recorded song CDs that accompany each unit of Firelight. Representing a variety of music styles, each CD features five songs by a contemporary Christian artist. Each song matches one of the Bible stories in the Firelight unit. These songs can be used to learn the story or to explore themes found within the story.

Recordings of songs, like those on the Firelight Song CDs, can engage kids in learning in a variety of settings. Play songs as people gather together. Introduce the entire story or important themes in the story as you learn to sing these songs together.

Engage small groups of children directly in learning by paying attention to individual elements found in the recordings.

Song Lyrics

Find engaging and age appropriate ways to present the lyrics.

Compare the lyrics in the song to the biblical text. What is missing? Was anything added?

Instrumentation

How does the style of the music affect the biblical story or give new insights into the story?

Vocal Interpretation

Does the vocal interpretation match the sense of the biblical text? Does Jesus invite or demand Zacchaeus to come down from the tree in the biblical story? Is that the way it is interpreted when it is sung or recorded?

Tempo

How does the tempo (how fast or slow the song is performed) affect the meaning of the story?

Silence

Are silences used in the music? How do they help tell the story?

Consider providing each child with Firelight Song CDs or suggest them to parents as gift ideas for their children. Kids will be able to continue exploring the songs and stories at home and share their ideas with their families.

Firelight Song CDs

God Feeds Us
Lost and Found

Multiply *(Mark 6:30-44)*
You Can't Take Away *(Genesis 27)*
Do Not Be Afraid *(Exodus 15:22–16:36)*
The Kingdom *(Acts 10:1-48)*
Elijah *(1 Kings 17)*

ISBN 0-8066-6427-4

Surprised by God's Grace
Jonathan Rundman

Well-Worn Prayer *(John 4:1-42)*
Seven-Color Promise *(Genesis 6-9)*
As You Did, Lord, at Emmaus *(Luke 24:13-35)*
Pass Us By *(Exodus 12:1-51)*
Treasurer's Report to Candance, Queen of Ethiopians *(Acts 8:26-40)*

ISBN 0-8066-6464-9

God Comes to Us
Peder Eide

Nothing Is Impossible *(Genesis 18:1-15)*
Who Will Come? *(Micah 5:2-5a)*
Family of God *(Acts 2:43-47)*
Let the Children Come *(Mark 10:13-16)*
Life on the Vine *(John 15)*

ISBN 0-8066-6444-4

Come to God's Party
Ken Medema

Come on In *(Matthew 22:1-14)*
These Are the Days *(Exodus 15:19-21)*
I Could Dance for a Week *(Esther 1:1–10:3)*
Before There Were Roses *(Genesis 1:1–2:4; Psalm 8)*
Zack, Jack *(Luke 19:1-10)*

ISBN 0-8066-6492-4

Let's Practice Faith
Celia Whitler

All and Me *(Luke 11:1-13)*
Open the Door *(Luke 10:38-42)*
Rest in Me *(Deuteronomy 5:12-15)*
All That I Am *(Mark 12:41-44)*
Forgive *(Genesis 50)*

ISBN 0-8066-6517-3

Peace Be With You
Thomas Ian Nicholas

Chat *(Isaiah 11:1-9)*
Hit Me *(John 14:15-27)*
Peace *(Matthew 5:38-48)*
Footsteps of Idiots *(Luke 19:45-46)*
Stopping It All *(Acts 9:1-22)*

ISBN 0-8066-6542-4

Examples of Sound Composition Charts

The following pages contain examples of sound composition charts for three Bible stories: the good Samaritan, the creation story, and "Jesus, Our Vine." They show just one way to chart out a sound composition. Symbols for each sound can be as simple or as elaborate as you want. Be creative! The important thing is that the performers of the sounds know when to play.

Refer to chapter 7 for ideas on creating sound compositions, and use these reproducible pages to spark the imaginations of your learners!

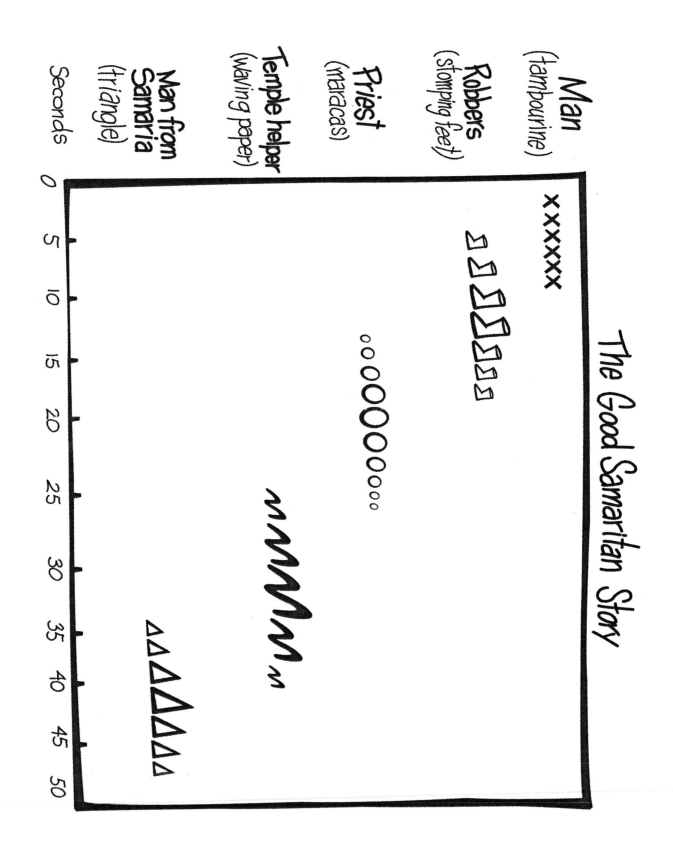

The Good Samaritan Story

	Seconds 0 5 10 15 20 25 30 35 40 45 50
Man (tambourine)	x x x x x
Robbers (stomping feet)	♫ ♫ ♫♫♫ ♫
Priest (maracas)	° ° ° ° O O O O O O ° ° °
Temple helper (waving paper)	∿∿∿∿∿∿
Man from Samaria (triangle)	△△△△△△△

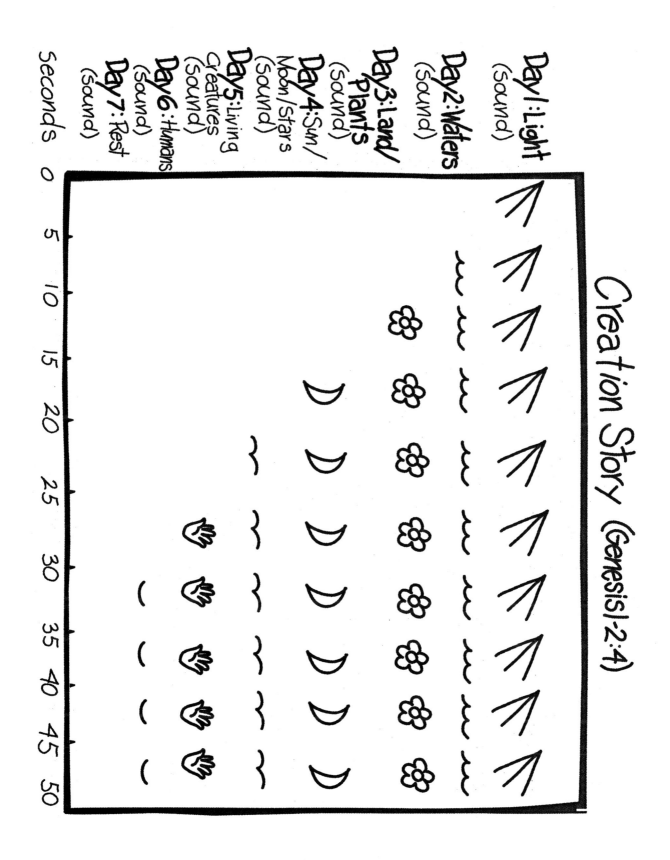

Creation Story (Genesis 1–2:4)

Day 1: Light (Sound)
Day 2: Waters (Sound)
Day 3: Land/ Plants (Sound)
Day 4: Sun/ Moon/Stars (Sound)
Day 5: Living Creatures (Sound)
Day 6: Humans (Sound)
Day 7: Rest (Sound)

Seconds   0   5   10   15   20   25   30   35   40   45   50

Jesus, our Vine (John 15)

Person #3 (sound)

Person #1 (sound)

Vine (sound)

Person #2 (sound)

Person #4 (sound)

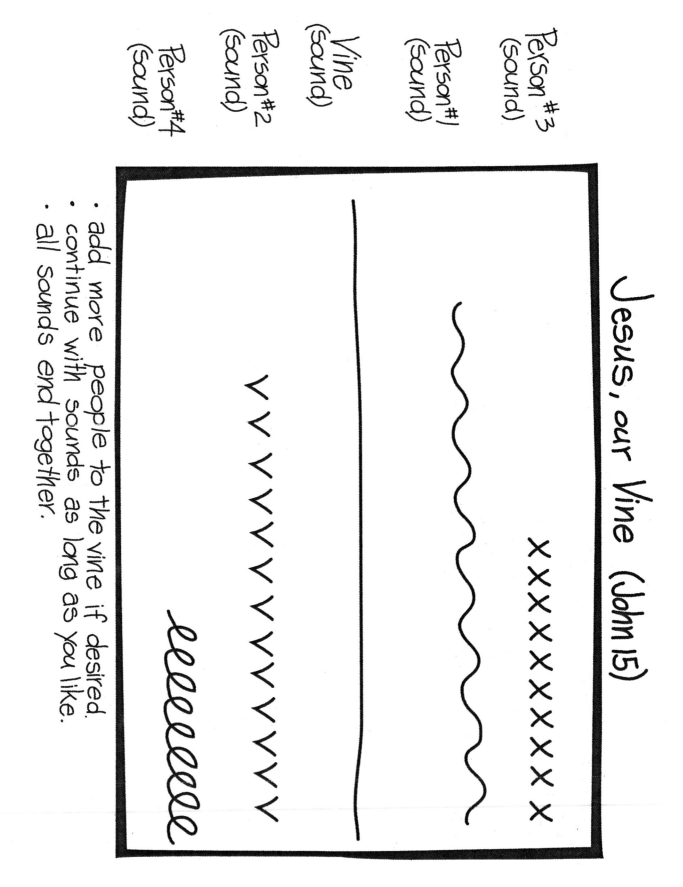

- add more people to the vine if desired.
- continue with sounds as long as you like.
- all sounds end together.

x x x x x x x x x x x

v v v v v v v v v v v v

eeeeeeeee